The Mind That's Mine

A PROGRAM TO HELP YOUNG LEARNERS LEARN ABOUT LEARNING

™

Materials created and written by

Mel Levine, M.D., Carl W. Swartz, Ph.D., and Melissa B. Wakely, Ph.D.

All Kinds of Minds

A Nonprofit Institute for the Understanding of Differences in Learning
and
The Clinical Center for the Study of Development and Learning
A University-Affiliated Program
University of North Carolina at Chapel Hill

In collaboration with

Parents & Educators Resource Center

A Program of the Charles and Helen Schwab Foundation

Have you ever thought about how your mind works?

Have you ever wondered...

- how your mind remembers how to spell a word or ride a bicycle?

- why you sometimes forget things?

- where ideas and feelings come from?

- if your brain is the same thing as your mind?

- how your mind solves problems and figures things out?

- if your mind helps you make friends?

- what imagination is?

- how your mind rests when you're sleeping?

- what's happening in your mind when you're having trouble learning something?

- if your mind is just like everyone else's mind?

In *The Mind That's Mine*, you'll find out how your mind works, what its strengths are, and what you can do to make it work even better!

Contents

Thinking About Thinking

Introduction

Do you ever think about thinking? It may sound like a strange thing to do, but it's really pretty important. In *The Mind That's Mine,* you'll find out about all the things that go on inside your head when you're thinking and learning. Once you understand how your mind works, you'll find out how you can help it work even better.

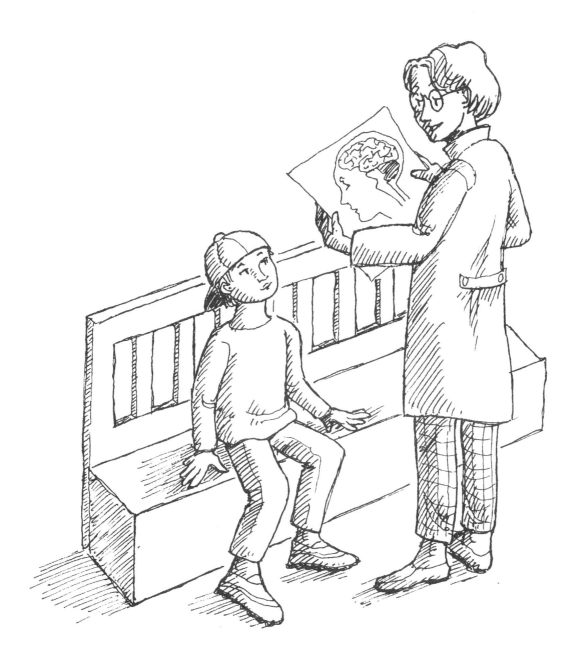

What's Inside Your Head?

Your **brain,** of course! Like your heart and lungs and liver, your brain is an organ of your body. It's actually part of your **nervous system,** which is like an enormous number of wires that connect different parts of your body to each other.

Your nervous system has two parts:

- Your **central nervous system** includes the nerves that are in your brain, brain stem, and spinal cord.

- Your **peripheral nervous system** includes the nerves that are everywhere else!

Throughout *The Mind That's Mine* program, you'll be looking closely at your central nervous system, because most learning and behavior in school gets controlled there.

A view of the inside of the Central Nervous System

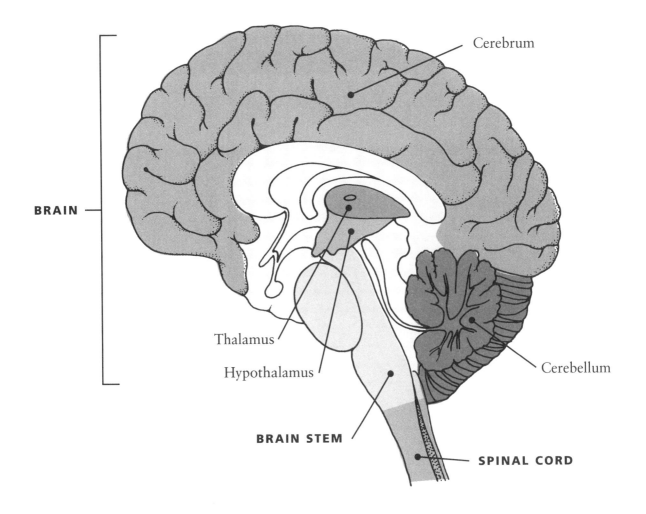

BRAIN

Cerebrum

Thalamus

Hypothalamus

Cerebellum

BRAIN STEM

SPINAL CORD

Your Central Nervous System

Your **central nervous system** is divided into three main regions:

- spinal cord

- brain stem

- brain

If you look at the picture on the opposite page, you'll be able to see where these three regions are located. You'll also see some of the brain's main parts.

What Your Spinal Cord Does

Your **spinal cord** is a bundle of nerves inside your spinal column, which goes down the middle of your back. It gets information about your body, and then it sends out signals to make your muscles move the way you want them to. It reacts to things like:

- temperature

- pain

- the position of your body in space

What Your Brain Stem Does

Your **brain stem** is just above your spinal cord. The brain stem works like an extension cord for some of your body's **functions** and senses, including:

- blinking
- blood flow
- breathing
- digestion

- hearing
- heartbeat
- swallowing
- tasting

Did you notice that your sense of smell does not go through your brain stem? It connects directly with parts of your brain. Can you think of a time when you smelled something that triggered an old memory? That's because smelling and memory are linked in your brain!

What Your Brain Does

Inside the protective armor of your bony skull is your brain. It's one of the most important organs in your body.

Take a look at all those wrinkles! The wrinkles are actual folds in your brain that help it fit inside your skull.

Your brain is made up of tiny nerve cells, called **neurons,** which connect with each other in many different ways. Scientists who study the brain think that there may be as many as 75 billion neurons in your body. That means there are more ways for your nerve cells to connect with each other than there are atoms in the whole universe.

Your brain's "wiring" is so complicated that no two brains are exactly the same. Even identical twins have brains that are wired differently. Let's take a few minutes to look at your brain and see what's going on in there.

A Quick Look Inside Your Brain

Your brain is made up of lots of different parts, and each one has a different job to do.

What Your Cerebrum Does

The biggest part of your brain, which is right at the top of your head, is called the **cerebrum.** The cerebrum is divided into two halves, called **cerebral hemispheres.** Although they look alike from the outside, your two cerebral hemispheres do very different things:

The main job of your **left cerebral hemisphere** is to figure out language and information that comes in or goes out in a particular order. Your left cerebral hemisphere also controls movement on the right side of your body.

The main job of your **right cerebral hemisphere** is to specialize in visual patterns, like pictures and faces, helping you figure out information that comes in all at once, like when you see someone's face. Your right cerebral hemisphere also controls movement on the left side of your body.

Just to make things even more complicated, each cerebral hemisphere is divided into smaller pieces, called **cerebral lobes.**

The Cerebral Lobes of the Brain

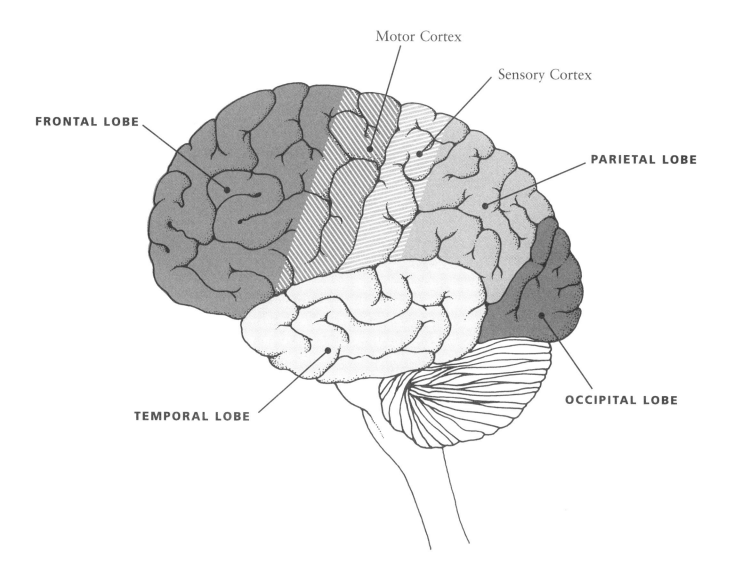

Motor Cortex

Sensory Cortex

FRONTAL LOBE

PARIETAL LOBE

TEMPORAL LOBE

OCCIPITAL LOBE

What Your Cerebral Lobes Do

Your **frontal lobes** are right behind your forehead. In some ways, your frontal lobes are the "orchestra leaders" of your brain. They help you find and use the proper part of the brain for whatever you're doing. They also help you control your behavior and emotions. The back part of your frontal lobe, called the **motor cortex,** works closely with other parts of your brain to make sure you move your muscles smoothly and accurately.

Your **parietal lobes,** which are located behind your frontal lobes, contain your **sensory cortex.** The sensory cortex receives information from your sensory organs, such as your eyes, ears, skin, and nose. The sensory cortex helps you figure out what different sensations mean and what to do about them.

Your **occipital lobes** sit just behind the parietal lobes. The occipital lobes receive information that comes in through your eyes. They figure out what you're seeing so you can tell whether something is on top of, under, or next to, something else.

Did you notice that your right cerebral hemisphere controls movement on the left side of your body, and your left cerebral hemisphere controls movement on the right side of your body? Pretty weird, huh?

Your **temporal lobes** are under your parietal lobes. The temporal lobes have a lot to do with information that comes in through your ears, such as music and language. Your temporal lobes are also one of the many places in your brain that helps you remember things.

What Your Cerebellum Does

Your **cerebellum** is at the bottom of your brain, in the back of your head. The cerebellum is responsible for fine-tuning your muscle movements. It can make you good at doing things with your hands or at playing a sport. A great football player, artist, or guitarist must have a super cerebellum!

What Your Thalamus and Hypothalamus Do

Deep inside your head are two more important pieces of your brain:

Your **thalamus** is like a great relay station. It receives all the signals from the lower parts of your body, such as your arms and legs, and sends them up to the higher regions of your brain. Every sense—except smell—goes up through your thalamus.

Your **hypothalamus** helps you control your appetite, your thirst, and the temperature of your body. It also has a lot to do with certain feelings you get, including angry and peaceful feelings.

The Mysterious Mind and Brain

Scientists who specialize in studying how the mind and brain work are called **neuroscientists.** Neuroscientists study the way brain cells "talk" to each other by sending out—and receiving—chemical messages.

Believe it or not, a neuroscientist can actually watch brains at work! They use **brain scans,** which are like videos of the inside of the brain. With a brain scan you can see what's happening inside the brain when someone is reading or sleeping or speaking.

Neuroscientists have learned a lot in recent years, but much about the brain and the mind still remains a mystery. Would you like to be a neuroscientist? Can you think of another job you could have if you wanted to help people use their brains better?

Different Kinds of Minds

As you can see, your brain is complicated. Besides all the work it does sending signals back and forth to help you control your body, there are also many different parts of your brain responsible for the work of your **mind**— for thinking and learning.

Although your brain is a part of your body, your mind is not. The word "mind" is used to talk about the thinking parts and jobs of your brain. "Mind work," or "learning," is done in many different areas of your brain. ▼

Different kinds of mind jobs are called functions. Here are some mind functions you might—or might not—be good at . . .

- understanding language when you listen, write, or read

- using language well when you speak

- paying attention

- remembering things you've seen or heard

- being good at something, like music or sports

- knowing how to fix something that's broken

- knowing how to get other kids to like you

How many things can you list that your brain helps you do every day? How many of these things does your brain do really well?

No one has a perfect mind. Everyone has some mind functions that they're good at, and some that they're not so good at.

Do you have a mind function that needs to get stronger? Trying to improve a mind function is like exercising a weak muscle: if you really work at it, it can get stronger and stronger.

If you have trouble with a particular function, that means you have a **dysfunction.** If you have a dysfunction, don't give up! There are lots of things you can do to help yourself. You can work around your dysfunction, or you can work on improving it. Do you do some mind functions better than others? Think about your friends and family. Can you figure out what mind functions they do best? It's important to know about your own mind's strengths and weaknesses—and to understand that other people's minds have strengths and weaknesses, too.

Technical Vocabulary in Topic 1

brain

brain scans

brain stem

central nervous system

cerebellum (sera-<u>bell</u>-um)

cerebral hemispheres (sir-<u>ee</u>-brul <u>hem</u>-is-feres)

cerebral lobes

cerebrum (sir-<u>ee</u>-brum)

dysfunction (dis-<u>funk</u>-shun)

frontal lobes (<u>frun</u>-tul lobes)

functions (<u>funk</u>-shuns)

hypothalamus (<u>hy</u>-po-<u>thal</u>-a-mus)

left cerebral hemisphere

mind

motor cortex (motor <u>cor</u>-tecks)

nervous system (<u>ner</u>-vus <u>sis</u>-tem)

neurons (<u>new</u>-rons)

neuroscientists (<u>new</u>-ro-<u>sy</u>-en-tists)

occipital lobes (ox-<u>sip</u>-i-tel lobes)

parietal lobes (pa-<u>ry</u>-i-tel lobes)

peripheral nervous system (per-<u>if</u>-er-al nervous system)

right cerebral hemisphere

sensory cortex (<u>sen</u>-sur-y <u>cor</u>-tecks)

spinal cord (<u>spy</u>-nul cord)

temporal lobes (<u>tem</u>-por-ul lobes)

thalamus (<u>thal</u>-a-mus)

In *The Mind That's Mine,* you'll learn about different mind functions and how they help you in school. You'll have a chance to think about how your mind is different from other children's minds, and how you can help your mind work better. Not only will that help you do well, but it will also make school a lot more interesting, and much more fun!

Paying Attention

Introduction

Every second of your life there are so many things you could be thinking or doing. It's your **attention** that helps pick out the most important things for you to concentrate on. Attention can help or hurt the way you learn and how hard you can work in school. In fact, paying attention is sometimes called **concentration.**

Sometimes, Paying Attention Is Like Watching TV

When you sit in a classroom, you can watch the teacher, your friends, the chalkboard, or the tree outside the window. You can listen to the teacher, the clock ticking, the noise from the corridor, or the ventilation system. You can be thinking about what your teacher is saying, about what you're going to do after school, or about the clothing that the kid next to you is wearing. There are so many things going on around you. How do you know what to pay attention to when you're learning?

In some ways, using attention in school is like watching television. To see a show you want to watch on TV, you have to tune in to the right channel at the right time. Not only that, you have to concentrate for the right amount of time, or you might not understand the plot of the show.

In school, you need to pay attention to what the teacher wants you to learn. Sometimes you may be able to listen and understand without too much trouble. But at other times, your mind may have to work hard to concentrate on important details, like the plus or minus signs in a math problem. It's really a matter of how you divide up your attention and when you concentrate on different details of a problem. When your attention is working properly, your mind is like a television set turned to the channel showing your favorite show.

Choosing the most important thing to concentrate on at the right time and filtering out the unimportant things are two ways attention helps you in school. But there are other kinds of attention that are just as important.

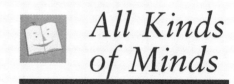

All Kinds of Minds

In the book, *All Kinds of Minds,* Eddie is a boy who has problems with his attention. Eddie is a great kid; he is fun and he has a lot of great ideas. But Eddie definitely has trouble concentrating. His mind gets distracted, and takes too many "mind trips." Also, Eddie keeps getting into trouble because he does things too quickly, without thinking or planning enough.

It Helps to Plan Ahead

When you have a project to work on, whether it's writing a report, solving math problems, or making a sculpture from clay, it helps to make a plan before you start. **Planning** can help your mind predict what a report will say before you write it, or estimate the outcome of a math problem before you start working on it. If you don't think your plan is going to work, you can think up another plan. In fact, you can keep planning different ways of doing your project until you come up with the plan you think will work best.

Planning usually works pretty well, but it takes time. When you're in a hurry, you may not take the time to think or plan ahead. Instead, you might be **impulsive.** An **impulse** is a feeling you get that makes you do something without thinking or planning. For instance, you might have the impulse to say something mean to someone without thinking about how your words might hurt that person. Or you might guess at a question on a test before taking the time to think about the possible answers. If you are impulsive, you sometimes act too quickly, without taking the time to make a plan. By slowing down and paying attention to planning, you can control your impulses. When you gain control of your impulses, you will do better in school.

Take the Time to Pay Attention!

It's important to pay attention to how fast or slow you're working. You're much more likely to get the right answer or do the best job when you take the time to pay attention to your work. Unfortunately, paying attention to plans and watching for errors in your work takes time. If you don't pay attention to how well you're working, you might work much faster, but you will make more mistakes.

Working at the right speed—not too quickly and not too slowly—plays a big part in attention. It takes time to concentrate, and it takes concentration to do things at the right speed!

Monitor Your Work

Sometimes, you even need to go back and pay attention to what you've finished! This is called **self-monitoring,** and it can be one of the hardest jobs of all.

A **monitor** is someone who makes sure things are done right and who reports back when something has gone wrong. In the same way, there are "monitors" in your brain that check what you've done so you can make corrections or changes if you have to. Before you hand in your spelling, for example, a monitor inside your head might go over the words to make sure they look right. After you do your math, your brain acts as a monitor to check your answers.

Stay Awake and Alert

Have you ever noticed how hard it is to pay attention in class when you're tired? Your attention works best when you're awake and alert. There are parts of your brain that actually control how awake and alert you are in school. Bundles of nerves in your brain stem turn down your attention at night so you can fall asleep, and then turn it up again in the morning so you can be alert during the day.

Getting a good night's sleep can help you be more tuned in during class each day. If you feel tired in class, you have to work hard to stay alert. Sometimes taking notes, repeating what the teacher is saying under your breath, or asking the teacher if you can get up from your desk can help.

Control Your Moods

If you are too happy or unhappy about something, it can be almost impossible to pay attention in school. When your moods or feelings bounce around too much, when you keep going from very happy to very sad, it's hard to pay attention. Controlling your moods can help you pay attention in school.

Control Your Body

If you're on the go all the time, if you can't slow down, how can you pay attention? You know what it's like to take a picture when you keep moving the camera—the photo comes out all blurry. Even a video camera has to move at the right speed for the tape to come out looking sharp. If your mind can't keep up with your body, you need to start thinking about ways to control your physical activity.

When You Have Trouble Paying Attention

Everyone has trouble paying attention sometimes. Most people can pay attention best to things that are fun and interesting. It takes more work to pay attention to things that are boring. But when students have a lot of trouble with their attention, we say they have **attention deficits.** They are often very smart, interesting people, but their problems with attention may result in some problems in school. ▼

When kids have problems with attention . . .

- they get distracted easily

- they get tired and bored when they try to pay attention (especially when working on things that aren't fun)

- they have trouble finishing their work

- they work too quickly without thinking

- they may move around a great deal and have trouble sitting quietly; some people say they're hyperactive

- they don't notice when they're making mistakes, or when they're doing or saying something wrong

Sometimes, people think that children with attention deficits behave badly on purpose, or that they don't do enough work because they're lazy. Really, they can't help it. It's not their fault that they have attention deficits. But once these children understand about their attention problem, there's a lot they can do to improve how well their attention works. Students with attention deficits may have other functions of their minds that work very well, such as memory, creativity, or imagination. They can keep using these strong functions to be successful in school, at home, and when they become adults. ▼

Do you remember all of the things that can help you pay attention?

You should try to...

- choose the right "channel" to concentrate on, at the right time and for the right amount of time

- filter out distractions by finding the best places and ways to work

- plan your thoughts, your actions, and the things you're going to say

- regulate your speed as you work

- self-monitor your work

- get plenty of sleep so you can stay awake and alert

- control your moods and impulses

- control how much your body moves around

- ask someone to help you improve your attention

Technical Vocabulary in Topic 2

attention (a-<u>ten</u>-shun)

attention deficits (a-<u>ten</u>-shun <u>def</u>-is-its)

concentration (con-sin-<u>tray</u>-shun)

hyperactive (<u>hy</u>-per-<u>ac</u>-tiv)

impulse (<u>im</u>-pulse)

impulsive (im-<u>pul</u>-siv)

monitor

planning

self-monitoring (self-<u>mon</u>-it-ur-ing)

No matter how much you pay attention, it won't help unless you remember what you're supposed to. Let's take a look at the different ways and things that you can remember, and how your memory helps you learn.

Remembering: Your Mind's Storage System

Introduction

Like other mind functions, memory is mostly a mystery. We know very little about where and how information gets stored in your brain. Yet we can describe different kinds of memory and how they get used in school.

Memory depends a lot upon two things: how long you need to remember something (length of memory) and what it is you need to remember (type of memory).

How Long Can You Remember Things?

Can you remember what you had for breakfast yesterday? Do you know what two plus two is? Can you recall what you got for your birthday last year? Some memories last longer than others. That's because there are three main memory storage systems: **short-term memory, active working memory,** and **long-term memory.**

Short-Term Memory

Short-term memory is for extra-quick storage. It holds only a small amount of information for a short amount of time. For example, when your mother asks you to do something, you store it in short-term memory, and immediately do what she asked.

What do you think happens when you try to put too much information into your short-term memory? What if you try to remember a long list of instructions that your teacher gives you about a project? There's a good chance you won't remember them all. If someone tells you a telephone number, you'd better write it down! Your short-term memory can only hold five to nine things for a brief amount of time.

Some children have problems with their short-term memory. They can go over something many times, but just can't remember it. Sometimes it's because the student isn't paying attention. Other times, it's just someone with short-term memory dysfunctions, and that student can still be very smart in a lot of other ways.

(Turn to the next page to find out how to help your short-term memory.)

If you want to help your short-term memory, here are two things that you can try . . .

Memory strategies are tricks that help get information into memory. For example, remembering the name ROY G. BIV can help you remember the order of the colors in the rainbow. The first letter of each word stands for a color: **R**ed, **O**range, **Y**ellow, **G**reen, **B**lue, **I**ndigo, **V**iolet.

Paraphrasing helps make information shorter. For example, a long explanation about how to do your history report might be remembered in a few short phrases: 1) Go to the library. 2) Look up the Civil War. 3) Write about the Battle of Gettysburg.

Active Working Memory

Active working memory is the system you use to keep several different things in your mind as you're working. When you're doing a math problem, for instance, active working memory lets you remember what you've done and what you still need to do. If you're reading, it lets you remember the beginning of the story when you're in the middle. If you're writing, active working memory helps you stop and think about how to spell a word without forgetting what you were going to write.

Some students have a lot of trouble with the parts of school that require active working memory. It might be especially hard for them to write and do math. They may even forget what they're reading while they're reading it!

Long-Term Memory

As you might have guessed, long-term memory is where you store information for a very long time, maybe even for a whole lifetime. Math facts, spelling words, vocabulary, and the names of important people and places all get stored in long-term memory. If your long-term memory is working well, you can find these facts quickly when you need them—on a test, while doing homework, or when trying to impress your aunts and uncles.

Some children have problems with long-term memory. They may find it hard to remember math facts or answer questions quickly and easily in class. They may have their biggest problems in writing because when you write, you have to remember many things all at once—like making letters correctly; using the right spelling, punctuation, and grammar; remembering ideas, vocabulary, even the topic you're supposed to be writing about. Some students with long-term memory problems just plain hate to write.

Here's something important to know: In order for anything to get into long-term memory, it first has to go through your short-term memory! So the things you do to help your short-term memory will be good for making sure stuff gets into long-term memory, too. But that's not the whole story. Putting things into long-term memory and finding them later on requires mind work.

As you go on in school, not only do you have to remember a lot of things, but you have to find them very quickly in your long-term memory. When you get called on in class, or when you're working on a test, sometimes you have only a few seconds to think of the best answer. This kind of rapid memory is called **automatization,** which means it's so fast and easy that it seems automatic. Can you think of things you can remember automatically? ▼

If you want to remember something better, you might want to . . .

- ask someone about memory tricks or strategies that can help, or make up some of your own

- try paraphrasing—then there'll be less to remember

- practice it over and over again (can you automatize it?)

- make up little games to test yourself, or have someone test you

- study just before you go to sleep

- think of things you already know that are like what you're learning

- put new information into categories (like all insects together)

- talk or think a lot about what you're learning

- make mind pictures of the things you're trying to remember

- use helpful tools—for instance, you can write down information, use a calculator to study math facts, or say ideas into a tape recorder

Can you think of how you might use these strategies, or what subjects they could help you learn? Can you think of other things to help you remember something? Are there some strategies you like to use best?

What Kinds of Things Can You Remember?

Can you remember how to multiply by nines? When you hear a song on the radio, can you remember the words? If you saw a shopping list, could you remember what to buy when you went to the store? Information comes into your mind in a lot of different ways—through your eyes, your ears, even your nose! The way it comes in affects how and where it will be stored by your brain.

 Visual memory helps you remember the things you've seen, such as the shape of a triangle or where you last saw your shoes.

 **Sequential memory** helps you remember things in the right order, such as a telephone number, the months of the year, or the notes in a melody.

 Auditory memory helps you remember things you've heard, like when your mother tells you to feed the dog.

 Factual memory helps you remember specific facts, such as the multiplication tables or the planets in the solar system.

 Motor procedural memory helps you remember how to do specific things with your muscles, such as tying your shoes or dribbling a basketball.

There are two ways to remember the different kinds of memory on this list. You can either remember the definitions, or remember the pictures that go with them!

 **Non-motor procedural memory** helps you remember how to do things that don't require your muscles to work hard, such as solving a long-division problem or remembering a cookie recipe.

 **Rule memory** helps you learn and remember rules when you need them, such as spelling rules, grammatical rules, and even rules that you discover yourself.

All Kinds of Minds

Bill is one of the children in the book, *All Kinds of Minds*. He has big problems with his memory in school. He understands ideas very well, and Bill is a superstar in sports. But he has trouble learning new facts and taking tests in school because his memory doesn't work too well. Bill gets so upset about his memory problems that he sometimes tries to act tough and then gets into trouble.

Sometimes, you have to use more than one kind of memory at a time. For example, if you repeat a joke you've heard, you have to use both your auditory memory (since the joke came in through your ears) and your sequential memory (so you get things in the right order).

It's possible to have a problem with one kind of memory, but be really good at another. If you have an excellent visual memory, for instance, you might always be able to remember the last place you saw your backpack. But if your auditory memory doesn't work as well, you might not remember that your friend told you where you left your backpack!

The Way You Remember Best Is Part of How You Learn

Everybody—even you—has memory strengths and weaknesses. Your memory strengths and weaknesses are part of how you learn. As you go on in school, it's important to know about how you learn best.

Technical Vocabulary in Topic 3

active working memory

auditory memory (<u>aw</u>-di-to-ry memory)

automatization (aw-<u>tom</u>-a-ti-<u>zay</u>-shun)

factual memory (<u>fack</u>-tu-el memory)

long-term memory

memory strategies (memory <u>stra</u>-te-gees)

motor procedural memory (motor pro-<u>see</u>-du-rel memory)

non-motor procedural memory
(non-motor pro-<u>see</u>-du-rel memory)

paraphrasing (<u>pa</u>-ra-fraze-ing)

rule memory

sequential memory (see-<u>kwen</u>-shul memory)

short-term memory

visual memory (<u>vi</u>-zu-el memory)

Memory never should work alone in school. It always needs to have brain partners that help it work better. Attention is one of your memory's partners. Language is another of your memory's partners. Let's take a look at how language helps you learn.

Language: Your Mind's Special Information Code

Introduction

Language is really a kind of code. But it's not a secret code. It's a code we all have to learn.

Most of what you learn in school gets into your mind through language. Books are full of language; teachers use language to explain things; you use language to show everyone how much you know!

As you might imagine, students who are good with language find school easier than students who have to struggle to use language well. When you grow up, there are a lot of great jobs that don't require super language ability. But when you're younger, you need to keep working on your language functions if you want to succeed in school. That's just the way it is. So let's find out more about language and how it affects learning.

From Sounds to Sentences: Putting Language Together

Sounds: The Smallest Bits of Language

Language is made up of sounds. But not all sounds are language sounds.

Language sounds are the sounds that make up words, like the sound /sh/ in "fish," or the /gr/ in "growl."

Non-language sounds are sounds that don't make words, like the sound of a cat purring or the roar of a lawn mower.

Your mind is very good at telling language sounds from non-language sounds. Your mind also helps you tell the difference between language sounds that are similar (like the words "mind" and "mine" in *The Mind That's Mine*). Your ability to figure out language sounds and tell them apart is very important for learning to read and spell. It would be hard to match sounds with letters if your mind didn't get the sounds right.

Some children have trouble with language sounds. They can be really excellent at many other things, but they have a lot of trouble when they learn to read and spell.

All Kinds of Minds

Sonya is a girl in the book, *All Kinds of Minds*, who has trouble with language sounds even though she is good at other parts of language. She is really excellent at art and at fixing things. But because of her problems with language sounds, Sonya has a hard time learning to read and spell. That makes her very sad.

Making Words Out of Sounds

In school, slowly but surely you build up your word networks. **Word networks** are huge collections of words that are attached to each other because they have similar meanings or definitions. For example, you probably use a lot of different words to describe people (like "kind," "mean," "cool," "weird," or "friendly"). In your word network, you remember how these words are like each other and how they are different. Then you can find just the right word when you need to use it.

Some students make excellent word networks; other students barely know what words really mean. How well you know words can be more important than how many words you know!

As you go on in school, you'll learn a lot of **technical vocabulary**—words like "denominator" and "photosynthesis." These are words you don't use much outside of school. The words in your technical vocabulary are words you use mainly in school.

Words are like friends; it's better to have a small number you know very well than a huge number you hardly know at all!

Some children have a hard time with the technical vocabulary they need to use in school. These students prefer using everyday words. You can't really blame them, but they still need to deal with the technical stuff for school. It's important. If you have trouble with the technical vocabulary you need in school, you can keep a dictionary of these terms, or draw word networks to help you.

Making Sentences Out of Words

Sentences are groups of words that go together and make sense. You have to use rules to put words together so other people will understand you.

Grammar is a set of rules for using words in a particular language. One grammar rule in English, for instance, is that we often add an "s" when there's more than one of something—as in the words "book"/"books," and "elephant"/"elephants." People who are good at using the rules of grammar have an easier time writing and understanding sentences than people who aren't so good at using these rules.

Syntax is a set of rules that helps us put words in the right order, so we say what we mean to say. The order of the words in a sentence has a lot to do with what a sentence means. Read these sentences:

"The boy that the dog saw ate three slices of pepperoni pizza."

"The dog that the boy saw ate three slices of pepperoni pizza."

In each sentence, who ate the pizza?

Making Big Chunks of Language Out of Lots of Different Sentences

Sometimes, language comes in more than just sentences. You might have to say or hear whole paragraphs, long explanations, or entire stories. It takes good attention, short-term memory, and active working memory to do well with big chunks of language. It also means you have to be pretty good with sounds, words, and sentences.

Some students have trouble when there's a lot of language. They get all mixed up when they have to read a long passage or listen to a teacher explain something at length. These students just can't seem to keep all the parts of language and meanings of words together in their minds. Can you think of things they might need to do? ▼

If you need help with language skills in school, try . . .

- sitting close to your teacher

- using your best attention skills when you listen in class

- asking questions if you don't understand something

- asking your teacher to explain something after class or after school

- talking! Be brave; practice as much as you can with family and friends

- reading a lot—reading can really help

- making charts and pictures to help you understand things better

- getting extra help from a speech or language therapist

Mastering the Language Code

Using Language to Speak and Write

Four ways you use language are when you . . .

- say something

- hear something

- read something

- write something

Speaking and writing are examples of **expressive language.** Expressive language lets you express yourself—by talking about something, or by writing it down.

Hearing and reading are examples of **receptive language.** Receptive language lets you receive information—through your eyes (when you read), or through your ears (when you listen).

Some students are excellent at both receptive and expressive language. Other students might have problems with one type of language but do well with the other. A person might be able to follow instructions and do a good job on something very complicated (using receptive language), but then she can't explain to you how she did it (using expressive language). Another person might be better at doing something if he can first put it into his own words.

If a student has problems with language, could he still do well in school? What other strengths could be used to make up for language weaknesses?

All Kinds of Minds

In the book, *All Kinds of Minds,* Eve is a girl who has trouble understanding and using language well. She is very quiet because it is hard for her to say her ideas. Eve has an excellent memory, and she is an extremely kind person. But sometimes Eve has trouble figuring out directions and understanding what she reads.

Language Skills

In school, you need language skills to do just about everything. If you have trouble with receptive language, it will be hard to learn to read and write. In math, you need language to understand the technical vocabulary, to figure out what the teacher is saying, and to solve word problems. You need language skills to learn a new language. You even need language skills in physical education class. Why do you think you need good language skills in gym class?

Social Language

Can you think of ways in which language helps people get along with each other? Language is important for learning, but it's also essential for getting along with others and making friends. This is what we mean by **social language.** ▼

It will help you get along with other kids if you can...

- get the right feelings into your language, so you don't sound angry or sad when you're really not

- know how to say things that will make someone else feel good

- be able to use language to fix a problem you're having with another person (like your mom or your friend)

- use humor in the right way for where you are and who you're with

- show feelings that go with the feelings of others (it's not good to say something silly when people are discussing something serious)

- be able to ask for something without annoying other people

- get good at speaking the language of others your age; use their kinds of words and sentences so you can fit in if you want to

Some children may be good with the language of learning but have problems with the social parts of language. Sadly, some of these students are unpopular because they don't sound right when they talk. They really can't help it. Their language ability just doesn't include much social language. What should a kid with social language problems try to do? If you had a brother or sister with this kind of difficulty, how would you try to help?

Language and Culture

The kind of language you use depends a lot upon your **culture.** Culture means a lot of things, including the way things are said and done in the country you come from or live in, the family you live with, or among your friends.

Some children speak completely different languages at home and in school. Other children speak the same language at home and at school, but use it differently in each place. Most children use a language with their friends that is slightly different from the language they speak in a classroom.

Dealing with language in more than one culture can be a real struggle, but everyone needs to recognize how valuable and interesting the languages of many different cultures can be.

Don't Worry, You're Not Crazy!

Have you ever talked to yourself? If so, don't worry. You're not crazy. Talking to yourself when you're working or solving a problem is actually a very important way to learn. Sometimes people talk to themselves so that they can understand something they are seeing, hearing, or reading even better. Some kids say they can't really understand something until they say it in their own words. That's probably true for a lot of people. Do you think it's true for you?

Technical Vocabulary in Topic 4

culture (<u>kul</u>-cher)

expressive language

grammar (<u>gram</u>-mer)

language sounds

non-language sounds

receptive language (re-<u>sep</u>-tiv language)

social language (<u>so</u>-shul language)

syntax (<u>sin</u>-tacks)

technical vocabulary (<u>tek</u>-ni-kal vo-<u>kab</u>-u-ler-y)

word networks

Language isn't the only way you can get information. Our next topic deals with other ways you understand and use ideas.

Solving Problems and Thinking Up Ideas

Introduction

Are you **creative?** Are you good at thinking up new ideas and solving problems? Do you notice what's happening in the world around you? No matter where you are, your mind is always thinking and planning, gathering information, and using ideas.

Where Are You?
Using Your Spatial Abilities

You already know how important language is: you can understand a lot from sounds and words and sentences. But there are lots of other ways information can get into your mind. One good way to get new information is by using your **spatial abilities.** Spatial information—information about the space around you—comes from ideas that often (but not always) get in through your eyes. Your spatial abilities tell your mind about how things look or how they fit together. ▼

You use your spatial abilities whenever you . . .

- decide whether something is on your left or your right

- recognize shapes (like triangles and rectangles)

- learn what different numbers and letters look like

- tell people's faces apart (so they don't all look the same)

- understand how the parts of things fit together (which is very important for doing puzzles, building models, and knitting sweaters)

- catch a ball, a beanbag, or a butterfly (but not when you catch a cold!)

People with excellent spatial abilities are often good at art. They may be able to build things well, or fix things when they break. Spatial abilities can also be very helpful in some sports. Which sports require a great deal of spatial ability? Which ones don't require as much spatial ability?

Some people learn best by using their spatial abilities. They'd rather learn by seeing than by listening or reading. In school, some information can be learned best by looking at pictures or diagrams or flow charts—or even by making up pictures in your mind!

Forming Concepts: Great Ways to Group Ideas

As you go through school, you'll hear your teachers talk about the important concepts in a book, on a test, or in something they're explaining to you. What is a concept? A **concept** is a group of ideas or things that go together and have a name. By using the name of the concept, you don't have to think about all the ideas or things in the concept every time you talk about it.

But that's still confusing, isn't it? Let's look at some examples of concepts, and see if that makes things easier.

Let's start with something simple—say, the concept of a square. To be a square, something has to:

a) be a kind of shape

b) have straight sides that are equal in length

c) have 90° corners (called right angles)

When you think of a square, you already know a lot about it. That is, you know the concept.

How about the concept of good sportsmanship? In order for people to show good sportsmanship, they should:

a) play according to the rules

b) accept defeat well

c) try not to act too boastful when they win

d) say good things to the other players

These are some of the things you might think of when someone mentions the concept of good sportsmanship.

You could learn the concept of good sportsmanship using words. How would you learn the concept using your spatial abilities?

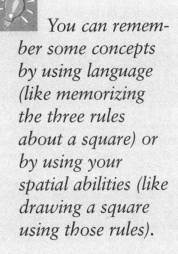

You can remember some concepts by using language (like memorizing the three rules about a square) or by using your spatial abilities (like drawing a square using those rules).

Let's try the concept of pets. To be a pet something has to be:

a) a live animal

b) an animal that won't hurt you

c) an animal that you can take care of

Perfect examples of pets include dogs, cats, parakeets, and gerbils. Examples that are not as good include grasshoppers, earthworms, and beavers. Really incorrect examples might be peanuts, hammers, and toenails! Sometimes it helps to understand a concept by thinking up good and bad examples.

Learning New Concepts

What's the best way to learn a new concept? You can:

- memorize the information

- make a picture in your head

- do both!

If you were just learning about squares, for instance, you could remember that a square (a) is a kind of shape, (b) has straight sides that are equal in length, and (c) has 90° corners. Or you could use your imagination to think about how a square would look.

Different Kinds of Concepts

There are may different kinds of concepts.

Concepts Can Be Concrete or Abstract

Concrete concepts are concepts you can actually see or hear or touch, or maybe even smell. A square is a concrete concept. So is a pet.

Abstract concepts are often harder to think about because you can't see, touch, hear, or smell them. Good sportsmanship is an abstract concept. Can you think why?

Here are some other examples of abstract and concrete concepts...

Concrete	Abstract
trees	happiness
airplanes	privacy
furniture	democracy
trucks	transportation
food	geometry

One way to tell the difference between an abstract and a concrete concept is by remembering that "concrete" (the stuff they make roads out of) is something you can easily see and touch.

Be prepared! As you go through school, there are more and more abstract concepts and fewer and fewer concrete concepts.

Concepts Can Be Verbal or Non-verbal

Verbal concepts are easy to think and talk about using words. Good sportsmanship is a verbal concept. It's easier to talk about good sportsmanship than to make a picture of it.

Non-verbal concepts are harder to talk about, but easier to picture. A square, for instance, is non-verbal concept. It's easier to picture a square than to talk about it.

Understanding Concepts

Every subject in school is loaded with concepts. Some people find concepts easy to understand and use; others find them hard. Some people go through school only partly understanding concepts. They may be able to use a concept (like fractions) without really understanding it. If you have a good grasp of a concept, you know about its different parts, you can use it well, and you can explain it to someone else. Can you think of some concepts you think you understand well? Are they abstract or concrete? Verbal or non-verbal? Are some concepts really hard for you?

Everybody has trouble with concepts in some parts of learning. You may be excellent at math concepts, but have trouble with sports concepts; you may be good at art concepts, but not so good at science concepts. That's part of everybody's unique way of learning—to be better at some concepts than others.

As you go through school, it's great if you can recognize **key concepts** while you're listening or reading. When you find one of these important concepts, slow down and think about how it fits with other concepts you know.

Here are some other examples of verbal and non-verbal concepts...

Verbal	Non-verbal
friendship	pineapples
practice	triangles
sadness	flags
knowledge	cars
dreams	parades

How can you tell a key concept from any other word? In a school book, key concepts are often printed so they look different from the rest of the words. Sometimes, they're in bold type **(so they look heavy and dark, like this)**; sometimes they're in italics *(so they look like they're falling over sideways, like this)*; sometimes they're ALL IN CAPITAL LETTERS, and sometimes your teacher will say, "This is an important concept to remember!"

Solving Problems: Dealing with Everyday Challenges

Every day, no matter where you are, there are always problems to solve. Problems aren't always bad: they can also be challenging and fun. You solve problems all the time, sometimes without even noticing them. ▼

You deal with problems whenever you...

- decide what clothes you're going to wear

- figure out what to write about in a report

- think about why people have wars

- figure out whom to invite to your birthday party

- settle an argument you've had with your best friend

- figure out what your team needs to do to win its next basketball game

You have to feel excited and optimistic when you're trying to find a solution to a problem. You need to keep cheering yourself on ("Come on! You can do it! Hang in there!"). Sometimes you have to be patient, too: big problems can take a long time to solve.

When you're solving a problem, try to use the systematic approach of a good problem solver. If you use good problem-solving skills, you'll do a better job. Poor problem solving can actually give you more problems to solve! Can you think of some examples of this? Could you write or tell a story about a person who got into trouble because of poor problem solving?

Problem solving is really important, both at home and in school. It's important to be a good problem solver as often as possible. Here is a list of steps good problem solvers use. ▼

To be a good problem solver you should...

- understand the problem you're trying to solve

- think about what the solution to a problem might look like (for example, before working on a math problem, you might estimate what the answer will be, or before planning a party, you might picture who could be there)

- plan how to solve the problem; don't be impulsive (remember that word?)

- think about strategies ("Let's see, now. What's the best way to do this?")

- do things in steps—one thing at a time—not all at once

- monitor yourself—that is, check how things are going while you're solving the problem

- use other strategies if, after monitoring, you decide the first strategies aren't working so well

- pace yourself so you don't work too quickly or too slowly

- know when and how to get help—from books, friends, teachers, parents

- learn from your problem solving so you can solve future problems

Being Creative: Doing Things Your Own Special Way

It gets pretty boring if everything you do is just like what everyone else does. Creative people do things in their own special way. ▼

You can be creative by . . .

- drawing cartoons or pictures

- playing imaginary games

- inventing new things

- inventing new ways of using everyday tools

- writing music or plays or stories

- starting a new club

There are lots of other ways you can be creative and original. Can you name some more?

One way to be creative is to do something called **brainstorming.** When you brainstorm, you let your mind go free and try to think up as many good ideas about something as you can. You might surprise yourself by thinking up things you never thought you could think of!

Sometimes, it's good to brainstorm with other people. That way, you can help each other think up original ideas. You can brainstorm to invent a new gadget, write a new song, or create an interesting character for a story. Try it!

Some kids hardly ever get a chance to be creative. They memorize things all day in school. Then they go home and eat hamburgers, watch television, do homework, watch some more television, have a snack, and go to sleep. There's not a lot of creativity in all that. The creative parts of their minds may get out of shape and never really grow much. Don't let that happen to you!

Technical Vocabulary in Topic 5

abstract concepts (ab-<u>strakt</u> concepts)

brainstorming

concepts (<u>kon</u>-septs)

concrete concepts (kon-<u>krete</u> concepts)

creative

key concepts

non-verbal concepts

problem solving

spatial abilities (<u>spay</u>-shul abilities)

verbal concepts (<u>ver</u>-bull concepts)

When you're in school, you learn lots of important facts.
You also learn new skills—different ways to do things.
Our next topic will help you find out about the skills you need, in
school and out.

Skill Building: How Your Mind Learns to Do Things

Introduction

When you were little, you ate everything with your hands. It worked pretty well, but it was kind of messy. Eventually, you learned how to use a spoon; then a fork. Later, you figured out how to use a knife. You learned to ask politely for someone to pass the salt and pepper, found out when to say "Please," and "Thank you," and "May I be excused from the table?" Today, you have all the skills you need to eat politely at the table. **Skills** are all the little tricks and techniques you learn that help you do other, bigger things. ▼

To learn new skills you have to...

- think that the skill is important to learn

- understand how the skill works

- know when and how it gets used

- watch someone else use it

- be willing to use the new skill

People who learn new skills often go through three stages:

- They're excited about learning a new skill.

- They feel angry or disappointed about not being very good at the skill, and needing to practice.

- They are proud and happy when they finally learn the skill.

Let's say you wanted to learn to play the guitar. You take guitar lessons, but find that you have to practice every night, which isn't much fun. You think maybe you should quit, but you stick it out. After awhile, you become a great guitar player. Wow, are you glad you didn't give up playing the guitar!

Skills Inside Skills

You learn all kinds of skills in school, from reading and writing skills to math and even athletic skills. Along the way, you also learn about studying and organizational skills. Like learning to eat politely, all of these bigger abilities are made up of lots of smaller skills called **subskills.** You need to be able to do the subskills well if you are to be good at the skills.

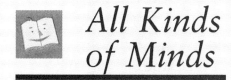

All Kinds of Minds

Some children can learn certain skills with incredible ease. Mario (Sonya's brother in the book, *All Kinds of Minds*) learns to read very quickly. He can describe words very fast, and he understands what he reads. Sometimes this makes Sonya jealous.

For instance, knowing how to read is a skill. Some of the subskills of reading are:

- figuring out the sounds of single words

- recognizing words quickly when you see them

- understanding what you read

- remembering and being able to summarize what you read

There are lots of subskills involved when you're studying, too. Some of them are:

- having good ways to memorize information and concepts

- underlining or highlighting important information

- outlining chapters

- taking notes during a lecture

- knowing how to test yourself before a test

- figuring out what you need to study

- thinking about the questions the teacher might ask on the test

Even when you play a game, there are subskills to learn. If you're playing basketball, for instance, you need to be able to:

- dribble
- pass
- shoot
- rebound

Can you think of other examples of skills and their subskills?

If you're having trouble learning a skill, it's helpful to try to figure out which subskill is causing the problem. That way, it's much easier to solve the problem.

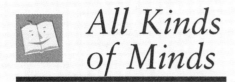

All Kinds of Minds

Derek in the book, *All Kinds of Minds,* is not good at playing sports. He can't seem to get his muscles to work properly when he tries to run fast or catch or throw a ball. Derek is a great student, but he sometimes gets very embarrassed when he has to take part in sports with other kids.

Getting Skills to Be Automatic

Remember when we talked about automatization in Topic 3? When you have an **automatized skill,** you don't have to think about it before you do it. As you get older, more and more of your skills need to become automatized. If you're so skilled with your math facts that you hardly even have to think about them, for instance, that means that some math facts are automatized. If you can form letters with a pen or a pencil automatically when you write, you've got letter formation automatized.

When there's something in school that's slowing you down, you might want to set a goal for yourself to automatize that skill. It may sound a little weird, but it can really help. Sometimes, when you can't do a skill automatically, you stop using it—or you use it as little as possible. Then it never gets automatized.

Why Do Some Students Have Trouble Learning Skills?

Students who have trouble learning skills are sometimes said to have **learning disorders.** It's important not to make fun of these kids, since they're already pretty embarrassed and often feel bad that they're having so many problems.

Almost all students have trouble learning some kinds of new skills. Some kids have a hard time learning to read, for example. They might not be able to decode language sounds. Or they might have memory or spatial dysfunctions or other kinds of language problems that can affect their reading. Students with reading problems are often very smart, but they just can't read well. They may learn better when they hear information—like listening to lectures or books on tape, for instance.

Other kids may be excellent speakers, but have problems with their writing. There are lots of different reasons why some kids have problems with writing skills. Some have **motor problems.** That means they just can't get their fingers to move well when they're trying to write. They may have good ideas, but their fingers refuse to cooperate. As a result, their writing takes too long or looks messy.

Some people can't write well because they're not good with language, or because they have problems organizing ideas. Other students have a hard time remembering all the subskills of writing, such as spelling, punctuation, grammar, forming letters, or even thinking up ideas. They can't remember all these things at once, so they hate to write.

Students who have trouble writing shouldn't feel bad or give up. There are all kinds of strategies that can help make writing easier and more fun. Some kids who have trouble writing find it easier to use a computer than a pen or a pencil. Others do best when they tell their story into a tape recorder before writing the story down.

Now that you know why some people have problems with reading and writing, can you think of some reasons why a person might have trouble with the skills and subskills of arithmetic? (Hint: Are there problems with attention or memory or thinking that could be interfering?)

Motor Skills: Getting Your Muscles Moving

Getting your muscles to work quickly and accurately is called **muscle coordination.** There are two different kinds of muscle coordination:

Gross motor skills control your large muscles, like the ones in your arms and legs. You use your gross motor skills when you skate, play volleyball, or ride a bicycle.

Fine motor skills control your smaller muscles, like the ones in your fingers. You use your fine motor skills when you play the guitar, type, or paint a picture.

In order to have good **motor skills,** you need to understand the spatial information that's coming into your mind. No matter how good your muscles are, you can't catch a ball unless you know exactly where it is in space. Kids who have trouble with spatial information may have a very hard time playing some sports. Playing baseball or tennis may be hard for them. But they might be great at swimming, running, mountain climbing, or bicycle riding.

You need good muscle coordination to catch a ball, draw a picture, knit a sweater, or play a musical instrument. There are people who have better gross motor coordination than fine motor coordination—and vice versa. ▼

If you need help with your gross motor skills (especially playing sports) . . .

- find one sport that you like and can get good at: you might be terrible at football, but great at golf

- ask an adult to help you practice when nobody else is around

- get some help from a coach or a physical education teacher

- see if you can participate without playing: maybe you can be team manager or umpire or scorekeeper

- exercise! Go on a hike or to a playground; keep your muscles working and your body healthy

Students who are good at most fine motor activities, but still have trouble using a pen or pencil, are said to have trouble with their **graphomotor function,** which is different from other fine motor activities. Can you think of ways that writing is different from drawing or fixing things, even though you still use your fingers for all of these things? ▼

If you need help with your fine motor skills (especially writing) . . .

- try different kinds of pens and pencils: one might feel "just right"

- ask for help: maybe your teacher can give you extra time or let you write less

- try using a computer; learn to type on a keyboard

- do things with your hands—hook a rug, fix a broken toy, play the clarinet

- practice! Write silly stories or funny poems, or keep a diary— just for fun

- use a tape recorder to record lectures, stories, or reports

Other children have trouble sensing exactly where their bodies are in space. They may lose their balance easily or not be able to run very fast. Yet they may be pretty good at bowling or archery or golf.

Still others have trouble remembering how to do things with their muscles: they have **motor memory** weaknesses. They may need to learn a sport where they don't have to remember how to do too many things. Such a student may be great at high jumping—or she may be great as the manager of the track team!

It can be scary and embarrassing when your muscles aren't working well. It's important to find the activities in which your fine motor skills and your gross motor skills are really good. It can make you feel proud, and, of course, it will keep your body in good shape!

Finding Your Talents: Your Fantastic Natural Skills

Do you have a special **talent?** Something that you do especially well? It's probably something that you love to do; it may have been pretty easy for you to learn. You might be a talented musician, a talented horseback rider, or even a talented leader. Everyone can be talented in some way. If you haven't discovered your special talent yet, don't give up! Keep trying new skills until you find it!

Technical Vocabulary in Topic 6

automatized (aw-<u>tom</u>-a-tized)

fine motor skills

graphomotor function (<u>graf</u>-o-motor <u>funk</u>-shun)

gross motor skills

learning disorders

modeling

motor memory

motor problems

motor skills

muscle coordination (muscle co-or-din-<u>ay</u>-shun)

skills

subskills

talent

Until now we've concentrated on the ways we think and learn. Another part of education, though, is knowing how to behave. In the next topic, we'll look at different parts of behavior.

How Your Mind Helps You Behave

Introduction

It's important to think and talk about behavior (including your own) so you can understand why people act the way they do. A lot of behavior skills need to be learned by your mind.

How to Control Your Behavior

When you control your behavior, there are three main things you need to do:

- Think about where you are.

- Think about the people you're with.

- Think about what's going on around you.

That information will help you consider the different ways you could behave. Then you can decide on the best one by doing something called **previewing.** That means you imagine the situation in different ways. You look ahead and say to yourself, "What will happen if I do this? What if I do that, instead?" In other words, you picture in your mind how people will react if you decide to do something.

Skilled behavior also requires self-monitoring (remember that from when you learned about attention, in Topic 2?). You need to watch and think about how you're behaving, and then decide if the behavior is appropriate. Ask yourself, "Is this going well? Do others feel good about what I'm doing? Do I need to change the way I'm acting?" And after it's all over, you might ask yourself, "How did that go? Did I act right? Is there something I should do differently the next time I'm in that situation?"

Let's try an example: Make believe that, while you're having lunch, another student says something nasty to you. Rather than acting without thinking, you stop and say to yourself, "Should I hit him? Call him a name? Should I ignore him or laugh or make believe I didn't hear him?" When you quickly think about these possibilities, you can preview and choose the behavior you think will work best. Then you can monitor the situation to see how it's going. You can always switch to another behavior choice if you need to.

(Turn to the next page to find out how behaving appropriately can help you.)

Behaving appropriately can help you . . .

- make and keep friends

- follow rules and stay out of trouble

- act fairly—called moral or ethical behavior

- accomplish things

- work well with other people

- feel good about yourself

Looking at Behavior Problems

A good way to study how behavior works is to think about some of the things that can go wrong with it. (We all sometimes do things we wish we hadn't done!) Let's look at some common behavior problems.

Impulsive behaviors happen when people behave without thinking, or act too quickly. Instead of previewing the situation or thinking about different ways to act, they do the first thing that comes into their minds. It's not really their fault; it's just the way their minds work. Their behavior could improve a lot. They should slow down and think about what they want to say or do before talking or acting.

Defensive behaviors are ways people act when they feel ashamed or embarrassed. For example, some children who have learning problems try to act tough to cover up the fact that they really feel dumb. They think no one will laugh at their learning problem if they act cool. Can you think of other examples of how someone might act badly to cover up something he doesn't want others to notice?

Conformity behaviors are ways you act so you can be like everyone else. Sometimes, it's fine to act like your friends. Everyone does it. But when you're afraid to be yourself—then **conforming** can be a real problem. Imagine someone who loves collecting frogs and toads, but decides to play soccer instead because the other kids think soccer is cool. Instead of doing what he loves to do, he's conforming to what other people think. What do you think about that? How much of a **conformist** are you?

Some people smoke or drink or use drugs or bad language just to conform, to be cool. They lack the courage to say no. Isn't it amazing that some people will wreck their lives just to conform?

Some people also worry a lot about their reputation. A **reputation** is what others think of you—sometimes for a long time. You can't completely ignore reputations, but if you spend all your time worrying about what others think of you, it may be hard to be the kind of person you want to be—the kind of person you should be.

Sad behaviors usually mean someone is feeling bad about something. People who are **anxious,** feeling worried or low, often lose interest in things. Sometimes they get extremely quiet. Some children might be worried about things going on at home or in school, or even in the world. Others may feel sad because they have **low self-esteem.** That means they just don't feel good about themselves. They may decide they're not good-looking enough or smart enough or skilled enough at sports. In reality, everybody is wonderful and unique. There are plenty of reasons to feel good about yourself—you just need to find them. Talking to an adult might help you work out your problems, or help you feel better about yourself.

Insatiable behaviors are ways kids act when they always feel the need for excitement. They stir things up and take risks with their behavior just to make life more stimulating. Students who are very insatiable get into trouble a lot. They need to find better ways of getting their excitement hunger satisfied. Can you think of helpful ideas for them?

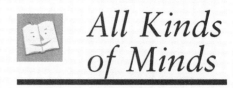

All Kinds of Minds

Three of the children in the book, *All Kinds of Minds,* have some behavior problems. Eddie gets into trouble for doing things too fast without thinking. He has impulsive behavior problems. Bill gets into trouble when he takes someone's wallet. He does this because he is using a defensive behavior to cover up his memory problems. Eve shows sad behaviors. She runs away because she is very sad about her language weakness.

Delinquent behaviors are very serious behaviors that can really get people into trouble. Sometimes people get into trouble just to impress their friends. Sometimes, when kids get together or join a gang, they feel too strong, as if no one can get them, and they can do whatever they want. Some kids become delinquent partly because they live in neighborhoods where there's too much violence. They learn to get into trouble when they're very young. They seem to imitate the older kids who are in trouble. Students who find themselves in this situation need to find an adult who can help them and keep them away from gangs.

Social Skills Problems

Some students simply don't know how to act with other people. If they have trouble with their social language (the way they talk to other people), they may say the wrong things in the wrong way, or talk about the wrong things at the wrong times. They may act tough or brag about how great they are all the time. Or they may have so little confidence in their social abilities that they become very shy and spend most of their time all alone.

Some students who have problems with their **social skills** get rejected by everyone else. They may have no friends at all because nobody likes the way they talk or look or act. It's important to realize that people with social skills problems want to have friends just like everyone else. But they have trouble learning how to do it—just like some people have trouble with their cursive writing or their reading comprehension. If other students make life miserable for them, it makes these kids incredibly sad. Instead, they need help and understanding.

Finding Good Ways to Deal with Bad Problems

Everybody has **stress** in their lives. You may face conflicts and bad situations at home, in school, or around your neighborhood. What's important is how you **cope,** or deal, with the rough parts of your life. Some students have terrible **coping skills.** When things aren't going right, they just give up, or get angry, or take it out on somebody else. Instead, they need to develop good coping skills.

Suppose you're playing baseball and you make a really bad mistake. Your teammates are disappointed and angry with you. How should you cope? Should you get angry and punch someone? Tell a joke? Walk off the field and quit, or try to play harder for the rest of the game? How would someone with good coping skills handle this setback? Can you think of times you've had some stress and used good coping skills?

Trying to Understand Someone's Behavior (Including Your Own)

It's possible to behave badly without being a bad person: some kids do bad things without meaning to. When people misbehave, you have to try hard to understand why they are behaving that way. Then you can help them stay out of trouble in the future.

You should try very hard to understand your own behavior, too. When you make a behavior mistake, you need to realize it and then try to figure out how to prevent it from happening again.

Technical Vocabulary in Topic 7

anxious (<u>ank</u>-shus)

conforming (kon-<u>form</u>-ing)

conformist (kon-<u>form</u>-ist)

conformity behaviors (kon-<u>form</u>-i-tee behaviors)

cope

coping skills

defensive behaviors (de-<u>fen</u>-sive behaviors)

delinquent behaviors (dull-<u>in</u>-kwint behaviors)

impulsive behaviors (im-<u>pul</u>-sive behaviors)

insatiable behaviors (in-<u>say</u>-sha-bull behaviors)

low self-esteem

moral (<u>mor</u>-ul) or ethical (<u>eth</u>-i-kul) behavior

previewing

reputation (rep-u-<u>tay</u>-shun)

sad behaviors

social skills problems

stress

We have now studied different aspects of learning and behavior. Our next (and last) topic has to do with your own unique mind.

Topic 8: The Mind That's Mine

The Mind That's Mine

Introduction

Congratulations! You've made it to the very last topic of your book. Did you notice that this section has the same name as the whole course? Can you think why? You've just finished studying many different ideas about how learning works. Now you can think about your own mind.

Different People Have Different Kinds of Minds

Even though everyone's mind depends on functions like attention, memory, and language to develop good learning and behavior skills, human minds are very different from each other. In fact, no two minds are exactly the same. Some minds work fast; others prefer to operate more slowly. Some minds can do a lot of things well; other minds, which are more specialized, do a few things well.

Different minds have different strengths and weaknesses. They also have different **affinities,** or special interests. Your mind might have an affinity for animals, for instance, or for outer space; other minds may love comic books, dolls, music, or sports.

Minds often have their own special ways of learning. Different minds learn things in different ways. Some minds learn best through language; other minds like to picture things and learn visually. Some minds like to use a lot of memory, while others try to do more through understanding. There are many different ways to learn.

It's really a good thing there are so many different people with different kinds of minds. In the adult world, there are many different kinds of jobs to get done, so we need lots of different minds to do them. An airline pilot has a different kind of mind from someone who raises cobras for a living. A computer programmer has a different kind of mind from someone who studies dinosaur bones.

Think about that the next time you run across someone who has a really different or unusual mind. She might grow up to be a famous movie star, or an astronaut, or an architect, or an opera singer. We should enjoy and admire all different kinds of minds.

Helping Your Own Mind Improve

Minds are like muscles: the more you use them, the stronger they get. If you spend all your time on **passive activities**—watching TV, talking on the phone, playing video games, or hanging around with your friends—your mind doesn't have to work very hard. It's probably not going to become as excellent as it could be. Like exercising to keep your body in shape, you need to keep your mind in shape, too. ▼

If you want to keep your mind in shape, you should try to...

- Work hard in school. Talk about ideas with your friends and family. When relatives ask you what you've been learning in science, for instance, surprise them! Tell them all about it!

- Find your affinity—something you love to do. Read about it, write about it, think about it a lot. Your interest may last a lifetime, and may even grow to be your job as an adult!

- Don't overdo activities that are too passive for your mind. Television is one kind of passive activity. Can you think of others?

- Be creative! Brainstorm with your friends. Write a play, design your dream house or car, sing a song, play the tuba. Be original whenever you can.

- Think about thinking. Not only should you use your mind, but think about how it works best when you try to do different things.

- Get to know people who have different kinds of minds. You never know what you can learn when you do things with other people. When you work well with other people, it's called **collaboration.**

- Be a teacher! Teach a younger child something new. Show someone how to play a sport or solve a math problem. Teaching is one of the best ways to build your mind. Everyone should be a teacher.

Motivation: Getting a Great Mind to Grow

Do you want your mind to improve and grow? If you do, you have to be **motivated:** you have to want to work for the things you want. You may have to do some things (like studying or completing homework carefully) that you may not feel like doing, but you know are important.

Students who are successful in school are usually good at **delaying gratification.** That means they can postpone having fun long enough to get some work done. They know that in the long run, their work will pay off.

Some students lose their motivation because they don't believe they can ever do well. After all, why try when you've already decided that you're just going to fail, anyway? Don't make that mistake! You're wrong if you think you can't succeed. Everyone has to find ways to stay motivated, to feel **optimistic** about his or her mind and how good it is. Every person's mind has excellent strengths. There are so many different ways to be smart that no one should give up on her or his mind.

Understanding the Mind That's Yours

Actually, you can't really figure out everything about your mind. For one thing, you have to use your mind to understand your mind! Then, you have to use your mind to think about how you're using your mind to understand your mind! (Try figuring that one out!) And don't forget that, as you grow, your mind is growing, too. Minds keep changing; they don't stay the same forever.

Minds are given different jobs to do at different ages. In kindergarten and first grade, for example, you need good spatial skills to tell letters apart. In fifth grade, you need to be able to remember a lot of things quickly for writing paragraphs and stories. As you grow and learn, you'll learn more and more new skills. Can you think of examples of how you need different functions at different ages?

Take a moment and think about your own mind. What kinds of skills and functions are you using right now? Where is your mind strong? In attention, memory, language? Where is it weak? How well does it do in various kinds of thinking, in skills, in controlling behavior? What kinds of special affinities does your mind have? Are your strengths becoming stronger? Hopefully, you and your teacher will find a special project you can do. Wouldn't it be great to show everyone what you have learned in *The Mind That's Mine*, and how well you understand your own mind and how it works best?

We hope you have enjoyed *The Mind That's Mine* program and that you have learned a lot from it. We also hope that you'll never stop studying the human mind, and thinking about the unique and wonderful mind that is yours!

Technical Vocabulary in Topic 8

affinities (uh-<u>fin</u>-it-ees)

collaboration (ko-lab-er-<u>ay</u>-shun)

delaying gratification (de-<u>lay</u>-ing grat-if-uh-<u>kay</u>-shun)

motivated (<u>mo</u>-ti-vay-tid)

optimistic (op-tum-<u>is</u>-tick)

passive activity

Glossary

abstract concepts (<u>ab</u>-strakt <u>kon</u>-septs) concepts that you cannot see, touch, hear, or smell, such as the concept of good sportsmanship (Topic 5, Page 39)

active working memory the memory you use to keep several different things in your mind while you're working (Topic 3, Page 22)

affinities (uh-<u>fin</u>-it-ees) special interests (Topic 8, Page 66)

anxious (<u>ank</u>-shus) worried or concerned (Topic 7, Page 59)

attention (a-<u>ten</u>-shun) parts of the mind that help you plan, self-monitor, stay alert, and pick out the most important things for you to concentrate on (Topic 2, Page 13)

attention deficit (a-<u>ten</u>-shun <u>def</u>-is-it) when someone has a lot of trouble with attention (not planning, not self-monitoring, not staying alert, and having trouble picking out the most important things to concentrate on) (Topic 2, Page 17)

auditory memory (<u>aw</u>-di-to-ry memory) the kind of memory that helps you remember the things you hear (Topic 3, Page 25)

automatization (aw-<u>tom</u>-a-ti-<u>zay</u>-shun) a kind of rapid memory where facts are recalled automatically (Topic 3, Page 24)

automatized skill a skill you can do automatically, without thinking about it (Topic 6, Page 50)

brain one of your most important organs, it's the control center for your body (Topic 1, Page 4)

brain scan a procedure which is like a video of the inside of the brain (Topic 1, Page 9)

brain stem the part of your brain that gets information from most of your senses and sends signals to your skin and muscles (Topic 1, Page 5)

brainstorming letting your mind go free and thinking up as many good ideas as you can (Topic 5, Page 44)

central nervous system the part of your nervous system that includes the nerves in your brain and spinal cord (Topic 1, Page 5)

cerebellum (sera-<u>bell</u>-um) the part of your brain responsible for fine tuning your muscle movements (Topic 1, Page 4)

cerebral hemispheres (sir-<u>ee</u>-brul <u>hem</u>-is-feres) the two halves of your cerebrum (Topic 1, Page 6)

cerebral lobes (sir-<u>ee</u>-brul lobes) parts of the cerebral hemispheres which are subdivided into the frontal lobes, parietal lobes, temporal lobes, and occipital lobes (Topic 1, Page 6)

cerebrum (sir-<u>ee</u>-brum) the biggest part of your brain, it is located at the top of your head and is divided into two hemispheres (Topic 1, Page 6)

collaboration (ko-lab-er-<u>ay</u>-shun) working together with other people (Topic 8, Page 67)

concentration paying attention while you work (Topic 2, Page 13)

concepts (<u>kon</u>-septs) groups of ideas or things that go together and have a name (Topic 5, Page 38)

concrete concepts (kon-krete kon-septs)
concepts that you can see, hear, touch, or
even smell, such as the concept of a square
(Topic 5, Page 39)

conforming (kon-form-ing) doing things
to be like everyone else (Topic 7, Page 58)

conformist (kon-form-ist) someone
who does what everyone else is doing
(Topic 7, Page 58)

**conformity behaviors (kon-form-it-ee
behaviors)** ways people act so they can
be like everyone else (Topic 7, Page 58)

cope to deal with all the pressures and
challenges of life (Topic 7, Page 61)

coping skills different ways to deal with
the pressures and challenges of life
(Topic 7, Page 61)

creative doing things your own special
way (Topic 5, Page 37)

culture (kul-cher) the way things are
said and done in the country you come
from or live in, in your family, or among
your friends (Topic 4, Page 34)

**defensive behaviors (de-fen-sive
behaviors)** ways people act when they
feel ashamed or embarrassed
(Topic 7, Page 58)

**delaying gratification (de-lay-ing
grat-if-uh-kay-shun)** postponing fun
long enough to get some work done
(Topic 8, Page 68)

**delinquent behaviors (dull-in-kwint
behaviors)** very serious behaviors that
can really get kids into trouble
(Topic 7, Page 59)

dysfunction (dis-funk-shun) trouble with
a particular function (Topic 1, Page 10)

expressive language the way you use
language to communicate information to
others (Topic 4, Page 33)

factual memory (fack-tu-el memory)
the part of your memory that helps you
remember specific facts (Topic 3, Page 25)

fine motor skills skills that control your
small muscles, such as your finger muscles (Topic 6, Page 51)

frontal lobes (frun-tul lobes) the
"orchestra leaders" of your brain, they
help you control your behavior and
emotions; they also help you find and
use the proper part of the brain for
whatever you're doing (Topic 1, Page 7)

functions (funk-shuns) different kinds
of mind jobs (Topic 1, Page 5)

grammar (gram-mer) language rules
that help us put words together so that
they make sense (Topic 4, Page 30)

**graphomotor function (graf-o-motor
funk-shun)** the skill of getting a pen or
pencil to move properly (Topic 6, Page 52)

gross motor skills skills that get the
large muscles in your arms and legs
to work quickly and accurately
(Topic 6, Page 51)

hyperactive (hy-per-ac-tiv) people who
move around a great deal and have
trouble sitting quietly (Topic 2, Page 17)

hypothalamus (hy-po-thal-a-mus) part
of the brain that helps control appetite,
thirst, body temperature, and angry and
peaceful feelings (Topic 1, Page 8)

impulse (im-pulse) a feeling you get that makes you do something without thinking or planning (Topic 2, Page 15)

impulsive (im-pul-sive) when you do things too quickly without previewing the situation to think about different ways to act (Topic 2, Page 15)

impulsive behaviors (im-pul-sive behaviors) ways people act when they do things too quickly, without previewing the situation or thinking about different ways to act (Topic 7, Page 58)

insatiable behaviors (in-say-sha-bull behaviors) ways people act when they feel the continual need for excitement (Topic 7, Page 59)

key concepts the most important ideas (Topic 5, Page 40)

language sounds sounds that make up words (Topic 4, Page 29)

learning disorders when you have problems learning certain skills (Topic 6, Page 50)

left cerebral hemisphere the part of the brain that helps you figure out information that comes in or goes out in a particular order; it controls movement on the right side of your body (Topic 1, Page 6)

long-term memory where you store information for a very long time (Topic 3, Page 22)

low self-esteem not feeling very good about yourself (Topic 7, Page 59)

memory strategies (memory stra-te-gees) little tricks that help get information into memory (Topic 3, Page 22)

mind the thinking parts and jobs of the brain (Topic 1, Page 9)

modeling demonstrating how to do a skill (Topic 6, Page 47)

monitor someone who makes sure things are done right, and reports back when something has gone wrong (Topic 2, Page 15)

moral (mor-ul) or ethical (eth-i-kul) behavior behaving in a way that is right and fair (Topic 7, Page 58)

motivated (mo-ti-vay-tid) wanting to work for the things you want (Topic 8, Page 67)

motor cortex (motor cor-tecks) part of the frontal lobe that works closely with other parts of your brain to make sure you move your muscles smoothly and accurately (Topic 1, Page 7)

motor memory remembering how to do things with your muscles (Topic 6, Page 53)

motor problems having difficulty controlling certain muscles (Topic 6, Page 50)

motor procedural memory (motor pro-see-du-rel memory) helps you remember how to do specific things with your muscles (Topic 3, Page 25)

motor skills skills that involve moving your muscles (Topic 6, Page 51)

muscle coordination (muscle co-or-din-ay-shun) getting your muscles to work quickly and accurately (Topic 6, Page 51)

nervous system (ner-vus sis-tem)
the body system containing the brain and nerves, which connect different parts of your body to each other (Topic 1, Page 4)

neurons (new-rons) brain cells
(Topic 1, Page 6)

neuroscientists (new-ro-sy-en-tists)
scientists who specialize in studying how the brain and mind work (Topic 1, Page 9)

non-language sounds sounds that don't make words (Topic 4, Page 29)

non-motor procedural memory (non-motor pro-see-du-rel memory)
helps you remember how to do things that don't require your muscles
(Topic 3, Page 25)

non-verbal concepts concepts that are easier to picture than to talk about
(Topic 5, Page 40)

occipital lobes (ox-sip-i-tel lobes)
part of the brain that helps you under-stand information coming in from your eyes (Topic 1, Page 8)

optimistic (op-tum-is-tick) staying motivated and positive (Topic 8, Page 68)

paraphrasing (pa-ra-fraze-ing)
a way of making information shorter
(Topic 3, Page 22)

parietal lobes (pa-ry-i-tel lobes) part of the brain that contains the sensory cortex
(Topic 1, Page 8)

passive activities activities that don't require you to take any action, for ex-ample, watching TV (Topic 8, Page 66)

peripheral nervous system (per-if-er-al ner-vus sis-tem) the part of the nervous system that includes all your nerves except the ones in your brain and spinal cord (Topic 1, Page 4)

planning a type of attention that helps you figure out what to do before you do it (Topic 2, Page 15)

previewing looking ahead and saying to yourself, "What would happen if I did that?" (Topic 7, Page 57)

problem solving the ability to understand a problem and figure out ways to solve it (Topic 5, Page 43)

receptive language (re-sep-tiv language) the way you use language that comes in through your eyes and ears (Topic 4, Page 33)

reputation (rep-u-tay-shun) what others think of you (Topic 7, Page 59)

right cerebral hemisphere the part of the brain that helps you figure out visual patterns; it also controls the movement on the left side of your body (Topic 1, Page 6)

rule memory the type of memory that helps you remember rules when you need them (Topic 3, Page 25)

sad behaviors ways people behave when they are feeling worried or low, or when they don't feel good about themselves (Topic 7, Page 59)

self-monitoring (self-mon-i-tur-ing)
thinking about how well you're working as you do your work (Topic 2, Page 15)

sensory cortex (sen-sur-y cor-tecks) part of the brain that receives information from your senses, including your eyes, ears, skin, and nose (Topic 1, Page 8)

sequential memory (see-kwen-shul memory) the kind of memory that helps you remember things in the right order (Topic 3, Page 25)

short-term memory the part of memory that handles extra quick storage: it holds a small amount of information for a short amount of time (Topic 3, Page 21)

skills all the little tricks and techniques you learn to help you do other, bigger tasks (Topic 6, Page 47)

social language (so-shul language) the ways you use language to get along with other people (Topic 4, Page 34)

social skills the skills you use to get along with other children and adults (Topic 7, Page 61)

spatial abilities (spay-shul abilities) tell your mind about how the things around you look or fit together (Topic 5, Page 37)

spinal cord (spy-nal cord) a bundle of nerves running down the middle of your back, it connects and sends out orders from the brain to the rest of your body (Topic 1, Page 5)

stress the pressures of living (Topic 7, Page 61)

subskills smaller skills that make up bigger abilities (for example, division is a subskill of math) (Topic 6, Page 47)

syntax (sin-tacks) language rules that help us put words in the right order, so that we say what we mean to say (Topic 4, Page 32)

talent something you do especially well (Topic 6, Page 53)

technical vocabulary (tek-ni-kal vo-kab-u-lery) words used mainly in school that are not used much in everyday life, such as "denominator" and "photosynthesis" (Topic 4, Page 30)

temporal lobes (tem-po-ral lobes) part of the brain that helps you understand and remember information that comes in through your ears (Topic 1, Page 8)

thalamus (thal-a-mus) the "relay station" of your brain, it receives and sends messages between your brain and the rest of your body (Topic 1, Page 8)

verbal concepts (ver-bull kon-septs) concepts that are easy to think and talk about using words (Topic 5, Page 40)

visual memory (vi-zu-el memory) helps you remember the things you have seen (Topic 3, Page 25)

word networks huge collections of words that are attached to each other in all kinds of ways (Topic 4, Page 30)